MW00881355

Portals Of Transcendence: Attaining Enlightenment Through Sacred Geometry And Ancient Symbols

Kevin Little

Introduction

Welcome to "Portals of Transcendence: Attaining Enlightenment through Sacred Geometry and Ancient Symbols." Within the pages of this book, we will set off on a captivating adventure into the realms of utilizing sacred geometry as a focal point for meditation and the transformative potential of sacred symbols. As we examine the complexities of this ancient practice, we open ourselves to new dimensions of self-discovery, inner growth, and spiritual transcendence.

The inspiration behind this book was born from a personal quest for a meditation practice that goes beyond the confines of contemporary or mainstream mindfulness tradition, which often place a primary focus on the breath as a point of attention. While recognizing the immense value of these practices, I yearned for a different path, one that would engage not only my breath but also the vast landscape of visual symbolism.

In my own exploration, I discovered that traditional breath meditation alone did not fully satisfy the depths of my spiritual longing. It was as if a part of me yearned to engage with the language of symbols and unlock the wisdom that lay hidden within them. This longing became the catalyst for this book, an invitation to embrace visual meditation as a profound tool for inner transformation.

"Portals of Transcendence" guides you on this path of exploration, bridging the gap between the seen and the unseen, the conscious and the subconscious. Through the power of visual meditation, we undertake a sacred journey to uncover the transformative energies of symbols and access the deeper recesses of our being.

In the chapters that follow, we will examine the ancient wisdom of various cultures, briefly exploring the history, meanings, and relevance of sacred symbols. We will discover the profound ways in which these symbols have been used as gateways to expanded consciousness, inner peace, and spiritual transcendence throughout the ages. As you turn the final pages of this book, you will have gained not only an exploration of the history, interpretations, and significance of sacred symbols and sacred geometry; but also a valuable set of practical tools and techniques to embark on your own transformative journey, the primary objective of this book.

By embracing visual meditation using symbols, we open ourselves to a world of infinite possibilities. We enter into a dance with the archetypes and universal energies that these symbols represent, transcending the limitations of ordinary perception. Through this practice, we tap into the wellspring of our own intuition, creativity, and spiritual connection.

Whether you are new to meditation or a seasoned practitioner seeking to expand your horizons, "Portals of Transcendence" provides a roadmap for engaging with visual meditation and exploring the transformative power of symbols. Through practical exercises, guided meditations, insightful teachings, and a collection of illustrations, you will be empowered to embark on your own journey of self-discovery and spiritual growth.

As we venture forth into the realms of visual meditation and sacred symbols, let us honor the wisdom of our ancestors and the collective tapestry of human consciousness. May this book serve as a guiding light, igniting the spark of curiosity and unlocking the profound potentials that lie within.

Prepare to explore the path towards enlightenment, where the power of symbols becomes a portal to the vastness of your soul. Welcome to "Portals of Transcendence: Attaining Enlightenment through Sacred Geometry and Ancient Symbols".

With deep gratitude,

Kevin Little

Chapter 1 Sacred Geometry: The Language of the Universe

In the magnificence of human existence, there is a language that transcends words, a language woven into the very fabric of the cosmos. It is the language of sacred geometry, an ancient and universal code that holds the keys to understanding the interconnectedness of all things. In this chapter, we investigate the profound history of meditation on sacred geometry, tracing its origins and exploring its significance across different cultures and epochs.

Section 1: The Origins of Sacred Geometry

Amidst the chronicles of antiquity, we find the earliest traces of sacred geometry as a meditative practice. From the intricate geometries etched into the pyramids of Egypt to the harmonious proportions of ancient Greek architecture, the foundations of this mystical language were laid. The earliest known origins of sacred geometry can be traced back to ancient civilizations that emerged thousands of years ago. While precise records are often scarce or fragmented, archaeological discoveries provide glimpses into the development and utilization of geometric principles for spiritual and cosmological purposes. Let us journey back in time to explore these fascinating beginnings.

1.1 Prehistoric Megalithic Structures: Illuminating Ancient Mysteries

Long before the emergence of written records, our ancestors left behind monumental structures that showcased a profound understanding of geometry. Gobekli Tepe, located in southeastern Turkey, is considered one of the most significant archaeological sites in the world. Its age has been a subject of extensive research and debate among experts. Based on current scientific consensus, Gobekli Tepe is estimated to date back to the Pre-Pottery Neolithic Period, specifically the 10th to 9th millennium BCE. This places its construction and use approximately 11,600 to 9,000 years ago, making it significantly older than many other ancient sites.

The monumental stone pillars at Gobekli Tepe are arranged in precise geometric patterns, including circles, arcs, and interlocking shapes. The design incorporates astronomical alignments, suggesting an understanding of celestial geometry. The layout of the ancient city of Teotihuacan, an ancient Mesoamerican city located in modern day Mexico and dated to the first century CE, exhibits geometric precision. The main thoroughfare, known as the Avenue of the Dead, aligns with celestial events such as the setting sun during the equinoxes, indicating a connection to celestial geometry. Megalithic sites like Stonehenge in England and the alignments of Carnac in France, dating back to as early as 3000 BCE, demonstrate a remarkable alignment with celestial phenomena, suggesting an awareness of cosmic geometry.

1.2 Ancient Egypt: The Language of the Gods

In the sacred land of Egypt, geometry held a deep significance. The Egyptians believed that the gods themselves governed the laws of mathematics and geometry. Their temple complexes and tombs were adorned with intricate geometric patterns, symbolizing the divine order that governed the universe. Meditating on these sacred geometries was seen as a way to commune with the gods, to seek spiritual insights, and to access hidden realms of knowledge.

1.3 Ancient Greece: Unveiling the Secrets of Nature

In ancient Greece, great thinkers such as Pythagoras and Plato delved into the mysteries of geometry, recognizing its profound connection to the fundamental laws of the universe. Pythagoras saw geometry as a pathway to spiritual enlightenment, perceiving geometric forms as embodiments of divine principles. Through meditation on these forms, seekers could unlock profound insights into the nature of reality and the interconnectedness of all existence.

Section 2: Sacred Geometry in Eastern Traditions

2.1 Hinduism: The Yantras of Divine Energies

In Hinduism, sacred geometry finds expression in the form of yantras—intricate geometric diagrams representing various deities and cosmic energies. These yantras serve as focal points for meditation, enabling seekers to align with specific divine qualities and to awaken dormant potentials within themselves. Meditating on yantras is believed to activate these divine energies, fostering spiritual growth and inner transformation.

2.2 Buddhism: Mandalas as Portals of Enlightenment

In the Buddhist tradition, mandalas serve as visual representations of enlightened realms. These circular geometric designs encapsulate cosmic forces and symbolize the journey to enlightenment. Meditating on mandalas allows practitioners to delve into the depths of their own consciousness, inviting them to transcend the limitations of the ego and merge with the divine nature of existence.

Section 3: Sacred Geometry in Modern Perspectives

3.1 Renaissance Revival: Harmonizing Art and Science

During the Renaissance, a resurgence of interest in sacred geometry emerged, as scholars sought to bridge the realms of art, science, and spirituality. Leonardo da Vinci, the visionary artist, scientist, and inventor, seamlessly integrated principles of sacred geometry into his work. He employed the golden ratio, a mathematical proportion of approximately 1.618, to create harmonious compositions in iconic paintings like the "Mona Lisa" and "The Last Supper." Da Vinci's exploration of geometric symmetry can be seen in his anatomical drawings and architectural designs, demonstrating his appreciation for balance and beauty. In his renowned work, the "Vitruvian Man," da Vinci showcased the relationship between the human body and geometric shapes, highlighting the connection between humanity and the divine order of the universe. Furthermore, he studied polyhedra and incorporated their mathematical principles into his understanding of light and shadow. Da Vinci's architectural designs were guided by the principles of sacred geometry, aiming to achieve harmony and balance in structures and city layouts. Overall, da Vinci's integration of sacred geometry in his art, science, and architecture exemplifies his profound appreciation for the inherent beauty and mathematical principles found in the natural world.

3.2 Contemporary Applications: Integrating Sacred Geometry in Meditation

In modern times, the practice of meditation on sacred geometry continues to evolve and find new expressions. Spiritual seekers and artists alike embrace the power of sacred geometric forms as tools for meditation, self-exploration, and personal growth. From the intricate patterns of the Flower of Life to the harmonious proportions of the Golden Ratio, these forms invite us to dive into the depths of our own being and to align with the harmonies of the cosmos.

As we journey through the history of meditation on sacred geometry, we recognize that this ancient practice transcends cultural and temporal boundaries. It invites us to explore the interconnectedness of all things, the unity that underlies the apparent diversity of existence. Whether in ancient temples or contemporary art studios, sacred geometry serves as a pathway to divine revelation, a language that unites the seeker with the infinite wisdom of the universe.

In the next chapter, we will explore techniques for engaging with sacred geometry in meditation, guiding you on a transformative journey into the realms of harmonious balance and spiritual awakening.

Chapter 2 Commencing the Sacred Geometry Journey: Techniques for Meditation

In the previous chapter, we explored the profound history and significance of sacred geometry as a meditative practice. Now, in Chapter 2, we begin a practical journey, exploring techniques that allow us to engage with sacred geometry in our meditation practice. These methods will enable us to unlock the transformative potential held within these intricate and harmonious forms.

Section 1: Setting the Stage for Sacred Geometry Meditation

Before we present the specific techniques, let us first prepare the space and create the ideal environment for our sacred geometric meditation practice.

1.1 Creating a Sacred Space: Designate a quiet and serene space where you can engage in undisturbed meditation. Decorate it with sacred geometry-inspired artwork, mandalas, or symbols that resonate with you, cultivating an atmosphere that supports your practice.

1.2 Establishing Intention: Set a clear intention for your meditation practice with sacred geometry. Whether it is seeking inner harmony, spiritual insights, or aligning with specific qualities represented by a particular symbol, clarify your purpose and keep it in mind throughout your practice.

Section 2: Visualization and Contemplation

2.1 Visualizing Sacred Geometric Forms: Choose a specific sacred geometric form that resonates with you, such as the Flower of Life, Sri Yantra, or Metatron's Cube. Close your eyes and bring the image of the sacred geometry to mind. Visualize it with clarity, observing its intricate patterns, proportions, and symmetry.

2.2 Contemplating Symbolic Meanings: Reflect on the symbolic meanings associated with the sacred geometric form you have chosen. Consider its representation of unity, balance, or specific spiritual qualities. Contemplate how these meanings can be integrated into your own life and spiritual journey.

Section 3: Breathing and Movement Practices

3.1 Harmonizing Breathwork: Begin your sacred geometric meditation by focusing on your breath. Take slow, deep breaths, inhaling and exhaling with intention and awareness. As you inhale, envision the sacred geometric form expanding within you, and as you exhale, imagine it radiating its transformative energy throughout your entire being.

3.2 Flowing Movements: For some practitioners, incorporating gentle and fluid movements can enhance the experience of sacred geometric meditation. Experiment with graceful movements that mirror the shapes and patterns of the sacred geometry you are working with. Allow your body to become an extension of the form, expressing its energy and essence.

Section 4: Meditative Reflection and Integration

4.1 Journaling and Self-Reflection: After each sacred geometric meditation session, take time to reflect on your experience. Journal about any insights, sensations, or emotions that arose during your practice. Explore the ways in which the sacred geometry and its symbolism resonate with your personal journey and inner growth.

4.2 Integration into Daily Life: Extend the impact of your sacred geometric meditation beyond your formal practice. Find ways to incorporate the principles and qualities represented by the sacred geometry into your daily life. This can involve mindful contemplation, setting intentions, or using symbolic reminders as a point of focus throughout the day.

As you explore these practical techniques for engaging with sacred geometry in meditation, remember that your journey is deeply personal.

Experiment with different approaches, adapt them to your needs and preferences, and allow yourself to be guided by your intuition. The transformative power of sacred geometry awaits your exploration and discovery.

In the next chapter, we will delve deeper into the specific sacred geometric forms and their unique qualities, guiding you on a meditative exploration of their transformative energies and spiritual insights.

Chapter 3 Unveiling the Transformative Energies: Sacred Geometric Forms and Their Unique Qualities

In Chapter 2, we explored practical techniques for engaging with sacred geometry in meditation. Now, in Chapter 3, we start our meditative exploration of specific sacred geometric forms, each holding unique qualities and transformative energies. Let us dive into the depths of these symbols, unlocking the wisdom they offer and allowing their transformative powers to unfold within us.

Section 1: The Flower of Life - Unity and Expansion

1.1 Symbolic Essence: The Flower of Life, composed of overlapping circles forming a mesmerizing pattern, represents the interconnectedness of all existence. It symbolizes unity, the web of life, and the infinite expansion of consciousness. Engaging with the

Flower of Life in meditation invites us to embrace the interconnected nature of our reality and expand our awareness beyond boundaries.

1.2 Meditative Journey: Enter into a meditative state, visualizing the intricate and interwoven circles of the Flower of Life. Allow its pattern to envelop your consciousness, guiding you into a deep sense of interconnectedness. As you meditate, contemplate the unity and expansiveness that this sacred symbol represents, and feel its transformative energy radiate through your being.

Section 2: The Sri Yantra - Harmonious Balance

2.1 Symbolic Essence: The Sri Yantra is a complex geometric design consisting of interlocking triangles within a lotus-shaped pattern. It represents the harmonious union of the divine masculine and feminine energies, embodying balance, manifestation, and spiritual growth. Meditating on the Sri Yantra helps us attune to the underlying harmony of existence and awaken dormant potentials within ourselves.

2.2 Meditative Journey: Envision the Sri Yantra in your mind's eye, focusing on each intricate triangle and its interconnections. Allow its symmetrical beauty to guide you into a state of inner balance. As you immerse yourself in meditation, feel the harmonious energies of the Sri Yantra aligning within you, balancing the masculine and feminine aspects of your being.

Section 3: The Metatron's Cube - Sacred Creation

3.1 Symbolic Essence: Metatron's Cube is a powerful symbol formed by connecting all the points of the thirteen circles within the Fruit of Life pattern. It represents divine creation, the bridging of the spiritual and physical realms, and the activation of higher consciousness. Meditating on Metatron's Cube awakens our creative potential, enhances spiritual connections, and brings forth harmony and balance.

3.2 Meditative Journey: Visualize the intricate web of Metatron's Cube, each circle and line shining with divine radiance. Allow yourself to merge with the energies of creation and transcendence. As you meditate, invite the transformative power of Metatron's Cube to

activate within you, awakening your creative essence and fostering a deeper connection with the realms beyond.

Section 4: The Vesica Piscis - Divine Union

4.1 Symbolic Essence: The Vesica Piscis is formed by the overlapping of two circles, representing the union of opposing forces. It symbolizes the divine feminine and masculine energies, the interplay of light and dark, and the birth of creation. Meditating on the Vesica Piscis helps us integrate polarities within ourselves, fostering balance, unity, and the realization of our interconnectedness with all aspects of existence.

4.2 Meditative Journey: Visualize the merging circles of the Vesica Piscis, the sacred space where opposing energies unite. Reflect on the harmony and interdependence of these forces within yourself and the world around you. As you meditate, allow the transformative energies of the Vesica Piscis to dissolve separations and guide you towards a deeper sense of divine union.

Section 5: Sacred Geometric Symbols - The Egg of Life and Cosmic Potential

5.1 The Egg of Life - Sacred Creation and Cosmic Potential: At the heart of sacred geometry lies the profound symbol known as the Egg of Life. Composed of interconnected circles, it encapsulates the essence of sacred creation and represents the boundless cosmic potential present within all things. Delving into the meditation practice centered around the Egg of Life opens a gateway to our innate creative power and allows us to connect with the limitless possibilities that the universe holds.

5.2 Embarking on the Meditative Journey: Prepare yourself for the transformative meditative journey that awaits. Find a tranquil space where you can fully immerse yourself in this exploration. Close your eyes, take a deep breath, and let your awareness settle.

Envision the intricate pattern of the Egg of Life in your mind's eye, with its overlapping circles gracefully forming an ethereal egg-like structure.

5.3 Embracing Cosmic Essence: As you bring your attention to the Egg of Life, feel a sense of reverence and awe welling up within you. Imagine yourself surrounded by the nurturing energy of the cosmic egg, enveloped in its transformative embrace. Allow yourself to sense the potent cosmic essence contained within its sacred geometry.

5.4 Awakening Creative Potential: Visualize the circles of the Egg of Life pulsating with vibrant energy, resonating throughout your entire being. Feel this energy awakening your own creative potential, igniting the dormant sparks of inspiration within you. Embrace the understanding that you hold the power to manifest and bring forth new ideas, experiences, and possibilities into your life.

5.5 Harmonizing with Cosmic Creation: Sense the profound connection between the Egg of Life and the cosmic dance of creation. Recognize that you are intricately woven into this tapestry, carrying within you the seeds of creation itself. Feel a deep resonance with the rhythm and flow of the universe, knowing that you are a co-creator, harmonizing your unique expression with the cosmic symphony.

5.6 Integration and Radiance: As you conclude your meditation, gently bring your awareness back to the present moment. Take a few deep breaths, grounding yourself in the present reality. Allow the transformative experiences and insights gained during your journey with the Egg of Life to integrate within you. Reflect on the cosmic potential that resides within your being, and consider how you can radiate this creative energy into every aspect of your life.

The Egg of Life unveils the gateway to our innate creative power and reminds us of the limitless possibilities that await our exploration. By embracing this sacred symbol, we tap into the cosmic potential that resides within and align ourselves with the ongoing process of creation. Embrace the Egg of Life as a guiding force, nurturing the seeds of inspiration and fostering the birth of new possibilities in your life's journey.

Chapter 4 Sacred Geometry in Action: Applications Beyond Meditation

In the previous chapters, we delved into the transformative powers of sacred geometry and explored its meditative aspects. Now, in Chapter 4, we expand our exploration to discover practical applications of sacred geometry beyond meditation. These applications invite us to integrate sacred geometry into our daily lives, rituals, and creative expressions, enhancing our connection to the divine order that permeates our existence.

Section 1: Sacred Geometry in Architecture and Design

1.1 Architectural Harmonies: Sacred geometry has long been utilized in the design and construction of sacred spaces, temples, and cathedrals. By employing precise geometric proportions and harmonious forms, architects create environments that resonate with spiritual energies, inspiring awe and facilitating a sense of connection to the divine.

1.2 Harmonizing Living Spaces: Bring sacred geometry into your own living spaces. Incorporate geometric patterns in your interior design, such as mandala-inspired artwork, sacred geometry-inspired furniture, or geometric patterns in textiles. This infusion of sacred geometry can create a harmonious and energetically balanced environment.

Section 2: Ritual and Ceremony

2.1 Sacred Rituals: Sacred geometry can be integrated into personal and collective rituals to amplify their power and symbolism. Create sacred altars adorned with sacred geometric symbols or use geometric patterns as focal points during ceremonial practices. The sacred geometry serves as a visual anchor, enhancing the sacredness of the ritual space and deepening the energetic connection.

2.2 Sacred Tools: Infuse sacred geometry into your ritual tools and objects. Carve sacred geometric patterns onto ritual candles, talismans, or ceremonial instruments. Each time you engage with these tools, you activate the inherent energies of sacred geometry, amplifying the intention and potency of your rituals.

Section 3: Creative Expressions

3.1 Visual Arts: Sacred geometry has long been an inspiration for artists. Explore your own creative expression by incorporating sacred geometric patterns into your artwork. Whether it is through painting, drawing, sculpture, or digital art, allow the beauty and harmony of sacred geometry to infuse your creations, conveying its transformative energies to viewers.

3.2 Sacred Jewelry and Crafts: Create or wear jewelry and crafts that embody sacred geometric forms. Design and craft pendants, rings, or earrings featuring sacred geometric symbols such as the Flower of Life or Sri Yantra. These sacred adornments not only carry the aesthetic appeal but also serve as reminders of the sacredness and interconnectedness of all things.

Section 4: Divination and Personal Growth

4.1 Oracle and Tarot: Sacred geometric symbols can be integrated into oracle card decks or tarot decks, adding depth and symbolism to divination practices. The sacred geometry present on the cards enhances intuitive connections, facilitating deeper insights and spiritual guidance during readings.

4.2 Personal Growth and Transformation: Engage with sacred geometric forms as tools for personal growth. Meditate on specific symbols that resonate with your intentions and aspirations. Allow the transformative energies of sacred geometry to guide you on your path, awakening dormant potentials, and supporting your spiritual evolution.

By exploring these practical applications of sacred geometry beyond meditation, we invite its transformative energies into various aspects of our lives. Whether through architecture, rituals, creative expressions, or personal growth practices, sacred geometry becomes a guiding force, aligning us with the divine order and awakening our innate connection to the greater whole.

Chapter 5 Egyptian Symbol Meditation: Unveiling Ancient Wisdom

In the rich tapestry of human history, the ancient Egyptian civilization stands as a beacon of wisdom and mysticism. Their profound understanding of symbols and their transformative power has left an indelible mark on our collective consciousness. In this chapter, we immerse ourselves in the Egyptian traditions of symbol meditation, unraveling the secrets and insights they hold.

Section 1: The Sacred Language of Egyptian Symbols

1.1 Symbolic Expression: Symbols held a paramount significance in ancient Egyptian culture, reflecting their deep spiritual beliefs and their connection to the divine. Hieroglyphs, intricate carvings, and art adorned temples, tombs, and artifacts, each carrying profound symbolic meanings. Engaging with these symbols in meditation allows us to tap into the essence of the Egyptian worldview and access the timeless wisdom they convey.

1.2 Key Symbolic Archetypes: Explore some of the key Egyptian symbols that are particularly potent for meditation:

1.2.1 Ankh: The Ankh symbolizes life and immortality, representing the eternal cycle of existence and the divine spark within each individual. Meditating on the Ankh invites us to connect with the life force that flows through us and find meaning in the eternal nature of our being.

1.2.2 Eye of Horus: Also known as the Udjat or Wadjet, the Eye of Horus symbolizes protection, intuition, and spiritual insight. Engaging in meditation with the Eye of Horus encourages us to awaken our inner vision, heighten our perception, and gain clarity on our spiritual path.

1.2.3 Scarab: The Scarab beetle is a potent symbol of transformation and rebirth. Its association with the sun and its ability to roll a ball of dung, seemingly bringing it to life, make it a powerful metaphor for personal growth and regeneration. Meditating on the Scarab invites us to release old patterns and beliefs, embracing transformation and the opportunity for renewed beginnings.

Section 2: Temple Rituals and Meditation Practices

2.1 Temples as Sacred Spaces: The ancient Egyptians revered temples as sacred gateways to the divine. These magnificent structures were designed to align with cosmic forces and facilitate communion with the gods. Meditating within the temple grounds, or even visualizing yourself within an imagined temple, can invoke the energies and wisdom associated with Egyptian deities and symbols.

2.2 Ritualistic Meditation: Egyptian meditation practices often involved rituals, invocations, and offerings. Engage in ceremonial meditation inspired by Egyptian traditions, incorporating incense, candles, and symbolic objects. Create a sacred space that mirrors the ambiance of ancient Egyptian rituals, allowing the transformative energies of the symbols to infuse your practice.

Section 3: The Inner Journey: Symbolic Visualization and Reflection

3.1 Visualizing Sacred Symbols: Choose an Egyptian symbol that resonates with you, such as the Ankh, Eye of Horus, or Scarab. Close your eyes and visualize the symbol with vivid clarity, exploring its intricate details, colors, and the energy it emanates. Allow the symbol to come alive within your mind, and feel its presence connecting you to the ancient wisdom it embodies.

3.2 Contemplative Reflection: After visualizing the symbol, engage in reflective contemplation. Consider the symbolic meanings associated with the chosen symbol and its relevance to your own journey. Reflect on how its energy and wisdom can guide you in your personal growth, spiritual insights, or daily life challenges. Allow the symbol to reveal insights and awaken a deeper understanding within you.

Section 4: Integration into Modern Life

4.1 Symbolic Reminders: Integrate Egyptian symbols into your daily life as reminders of the wisdom and insights gained through meditation. Wear jewelry or clothing adorned with Egyptian motifs, place symbolic artifacts in your living space, or create artwork inspired by Egyptian symbols. These symbolic reminders serve as anchors, inviting you to align with the transformative energies and carry the wisdom into every aspect of your existence.

4.2 Embodying Egyptian Wisdom: Embrace the values and teachings embodied in Egyptian symbols. Emulate the qualities of the Ankh, Eye of Horus, or Scarab in your interactions and choices. Infuse your actions with life-affirming energy, trust your intuition, and embrace the transformative power of personal growth and rebirth.

As we delve into the Egyptian traditions of symbol meditation, we unlock ancient wisdom and connect with the vibrant tapestry of their spiritual legacy. Through engaging with the sacred symbols of this extraordinary civilization, we embrace a deeper understanding of ourselves and the universe. May the Egyptian symbols guide and inspire you on your meditative journey, unraveling the mysteries of existence and empowering your spiritual growth.

In the next chapter, we will broaden our exploration to encompass other cultural traditions of symbol meditation, uncovering the diverse ways in which symbols have been utilized as vehicles for inner transformation throughout history.

Chapter 6 Symbol Meditation Across Cultures: Exploring Diverse Paths of Inner Transformation

In this chapter, we examine various cultural traditions, each weaving a unique tapestry of symbol meditation. From ancient civilizations to indigenous cultures, we uncover the diverse ways in which symbols have been utilized as vehicles for inner transformation throughout history. Let us delve into these rich traditions and explore the transformative power of symbols across different cultures.

Section 1: Native American Symbol Meditation

1.1 Sacred Petroglyphs and Pictographs: Native American cultures have a long-standing tradition of utilizing symbols for meditation and spiritual connection. Petroglyphs, rock carvings, and pictographs, found in various landscapes, carry profound symbolic meanings. Engaging with these symbols in meditation allows us to connect with the wisdom of the land and tap into the ancestral energies.

1.2 Medicine Wheels and Mandalas: Medicine wheels and mandalas are sacred circular formations that serve as focal points for meditation and spiritual exploration. Native American tribes, such as the Lakota and the Navajo, utilize these symbolic structures to facilitate balance, healing, and connection with the natural world. Engaging with medicine wheels and mandalas in meditation aligns us with the cycles of nature and invites transformative experiences.

Section 2: East Asian Symbol Meditation

2.1 Buddhist Mudras and Yantras: In East Asian cultures, such as those influenced by Buddhism, symbols play a significant role in meditation. Mudras, hand gestures with symbolic meanings, are employed to channel energy and facilitate inner transformation. Yantras, geometric diagrams with specific symbolic qualities, are visualized or utilized as objects of focus, inviting deep contemplation and awakening.

2.2 Taoist Tai Chi and Calligraphy: Taoist traditions embrace the meditative power of movement and calligraphy. Tai Chi, a martial art often practiced as a moving meditation, embodies the principles of yin and yang and invites practitioners to harmonize body, mind, and spirit. Calligraphy, with its brush strokes and intentional ink patterns, serves as a meditative practice that embodies the essence of Taoist philosophy and allows for self-expression and contemplation.

Section 3: Indigenous Symbol Meditation

3.1 Australian Aboriginal Dreamtime Symbols: Indigenous cultures, such as the Australian Aboriginals, hold profound wisdom in their symbolism. Dreamtime symbols, found in their artwork and stories, represent the interconnectedness of land, spirit, and culture. Engaging with these symbols through meditation connects us to the timeless wisdom of indigenous traditions, fostering a deep respect for the natural world and the ancestral spirits.

3.2 Maori Koru and Ta Moko: The Maori people of New Zealand employ the Koru, a spiral-shaped symbol, as a representation of new beginnings, growth, and connection to their ancestral heritage. Ta Moko,

traditional Maori tattooing, embodies powerful symbolism and serves as a meditation on personal identity, cultural belonging, and spiritual transformation.

Section 4: Symbol Meditation in Esoteric Traditions

4.1 Hermeticism and Alchemical Symbols: Esoteric traditions, such as Hermeticism and alchemy, utilize symbols as keys to unlock inner transformation and spiritual realization. Symbols like the Caduceus, the Tree of Life, and the Ouroboros hold deep esoteric meanings. Engaging with these symbols in meditation invites seekers to explore the depths of their consciousness, alchemically transmuting the self and attaining higher states of awareness.

4.2 Celtic Ogham and Knotwork: Celtic cultures incorporate symbols, such as Ogham writing and intricate knotwork, as vehicles for meditation and connection to their ancestral heritage. Ogham, a system of ancient Celtic symbols carved into trees, serves as a tool for contemplation and communication with the natural world. Celtic knotwork, with its interlacing patterns, invites meditative reflection on the interconnectedness of all things.

As we explore these diverse cultural traditions of symbol meditation, we recognize the universal language of symbols and their capacity to awaken transformative experiences within us. Each tradition offers a unique perspective and approach, enriching our understanding of the profound impact symbols have had on humanity's spiritual evolution. May these insights inspire you to explore the depths of symbol meditation and discover the transformative power that awaits within these timeless symbols.

Chapter 7 Mandalas: The Sacred Gateway to Inner Harmony and Wholeness

Mandalas have been revered across cultures and throughout history as powerful tools for meditation and self-exploration. In this chapter, we delve into the enchanting world of mandala meditation. We explore the origins, symbolism, and transformative qualities of mandalas, and guide you in harnessing their inherent power to find inner harmony and wholeness.

Section 1: The Essence of Mandalas

1.1 Origins and Cultural Significance: Mandalas, derived from the Sanskrit word for "circle," have a rich history spanning numerous cultures, including Hinduism, Buddhism, Native American traditions, and more. They represent the interconnectedness of all things and serve as potent symbols of unity and cosmic order.

1.2 Symbolic Elements: Mandalas typically consist of intricate geometric patterns and symbols arranged around a central focal point. These patterns embody sacred geometry, incorporating circles, squares, triangles, and other shapes that evoke a sense of balance, symmetry, and harmony.

Section 2: Engaging in Mandala Meditation

2.1 Setting the Space: Create a serene and comfortable space for your mandala meditation practice. Choose a quiet area where you can sit undisturbed, and consider placing a physical mandala or mandala artwork in your line of sight for enhanced focus.

2.2 Seating and Posture: Find a seated position that promotes both relaxation and alertness. Sit on a cushion or a chair, ensuring your spine is upright and your body is at ease. Rest your hands comfortably in your lap or adopt a mudra that resonates with your intention.

Section 3: Focusing and Centering

3.1 Gazing or Visualization: Begin your mandala meditation by softly gazing at the central focal point of the mandala. If using a physical mandala, allow your eyes to wander along the intricate patterns, gradually bringing your attention to the center. If visualizing a mandala, gently close your eyes and visualize the mandala in your mind's eye, inviting its vibrant colors and intricate details to come alive.

3.2 Breath Awareness: Shift your focus to your breath, observing its natural rhythm and flow. Take deep, conscious breaths, inhaling through your nose and exhaling through your mouth. With each breath, let go of any tension or distractions, and allow yourself to enter a state of deep relaxation and receptivity.

Section 4: Journeying Within the Mandala

4.1 Exploration and Reflection: As you continue to engage with the mandala, allow your attention to move along its intricate patterns and shapes. Explore the details with a sense of curiosity, observing any thoughts, feelings, or sensations that arise. Reflect on the symbolism

of the mandala, considering how it relates to your personal journey and the areas of your life where you seek harmony and wholeness.

4.2 Expressive Creation: To deepen your connection with mandalas, you can also engage in creating your own mandalas. Use various art materials such as colored pencils, paints, or digital tools to design your unique mandala. This process allows for self-expression and provides a deeper understanding of the transformative qualities of mandalas.

Section 5: Integration and Reflection

5.1 Closing and Grounding: As you conclude your mandala meditation, take a few moments to ground yourself. Bring your attention back to your breath, feeling the sensation of your body in the present moment. Express gratitude for the experience and the wisdom gained through your engagement with the mandala.

5.2 Reflection and Journaling: After your meditation, spend some time journaling or reflecting on your experience. Write about any insights, emotions, or messages that emerged during your meditation. Explore how the mandala's symbolism and energy relate to your journey of inner harmony and wholeness.

Mandala meditation offers a profound path to explore the depths of your being, cultivating inner harmony and embracing the interconnectedness of all things. As you continue your journey with mandalas, may they guide you towards a state of balance, unity, and transformation.

In the next chapter, we will embark on an exploration of specific types of mandalas and their unique qualities, allowing you to further deepen your understanding and engagement with these sacred symbols.

Chapter 8 Exploring the Kaleidoscope of Mandalas: Unveiling Their Unique Qualities

In this chapter, we will explore specific types of mandalas, each offering its own unique qualities and transformative potential. From traditional mandalas to specialized variations, we uncover the kaleidoscope of mandalas, inviting you to deepen your understanding and engagement with these sacred symbols.

Section 1: Traditional Mandalas

1.1 Tibetan Buddhist Mandalas: Tibetan Buddhist mandalas are intricate and vibrant, often depicting deities and cosmological elements. These mandalas symbolize the sacred universe and serve as visual aids for spiritual practice and meditation. Engaging with Tibetan Buddhist mandalas invites connection with the enlightened qualities embodied by the deities and the cosmic order they represent.

1.2 Hindu Yantras: Yantras are geometric mandalas used in Hindu traditions for meditation and worship. These precise and symmetrical patterns represent specific deities and embody their divine energies. By meditating on Hindu yantras, one can awaken and align with the qualities and blessings associated with the respective deities.

Section 2: Nature-Inspired Mandalas

2.1 Flower Mandalas: Flower mandalas are created using various types of flowers and petals arranged in symmetrical patterns. These mandalas symbolize the beauty, impermanence, and interconnectedness of all living beings. Meditating on flower mandalas cultivates an appreciation for the transient nature of life and awakens a deep sense of interconnectedness with the natural world.

2.2 Tree of Life Mandalas: Inspired by the ancient concept of the Tree of Life found in various cultures, these mandalas depict a tree with its roots reaching into the earth and its branches reaching towards the sky. Tree of Life mandalas symbolize the interplay between the physical and spiritual realms, inviting a deep connection with the cycles of life, growth, and transformation.

Section 3: Healing Mandalas

3.1 Chakra Mandalas: Chakra mandalas incorporate the seven main energy centers in the body, known as chakras. Each chakra is represented by a specific color and symbolizes different aspects of our physical, emotional, and spiritual well-being. Meditating on chakra mandalas helps to balance and align these energy centers, promoting overall harmony and healing.

3.2 Crystal Mandalas: Crystal mandalas utilize the vibrational properties of crystals and gemstones to create sacred geometric patterns. Each crystal carries unique energetic qualities, and by working with crystal mandalas in meditation, one can harness the healing and transformative energies of these gemstones, promoting balance and alignment on multiple levels.

Section 4: Personal Expression Mandalas

4.1 Intention Mandalas: Intention mandalas are personalized mandalas created with specific intentions and affirmations. By infusing the mandala with symbols, colors, and words that represent one's intentions, a powerful energy is generated. Meditating on intention mandalas helps to align one's focus and energy towards the desired outcome, amplifying the manifestation process.

4.2 Journey Mandalas: Journey mandalas are created to capture and represent personal growth and transformative experiences. They serve as visual narratives of an individual's journey, depicting significant events, emotions, and insights. Meditating on journey mandalas allows for reflection, integration, and a deeper understanding of one's unique path.

Section 5: Sacred Geometry Mandalas

5.1 Fractal Mandalas: Fractal mandalas are intricate, self-repeating geometric patterns that reveal infinite complexity. They embody the concept of the "as above, so below," reflecting the interconnectedness and self-similarity found throughout the universe. Meditating on fractal mandalas invites contemplation of the infinite nature of existence and the interconnectedness of all things.

5.2 Labyrinth Mandalas: Labyrinth mandalas incorporate labyrinthine paths that lead to a central point. Walking or visually tracing a labyrinth mandala can induce a meditative state and encourage introspection, symbolizing the journey to the center of oneself. Meditating on labyrinth mandalas invites self-reflection, contemplation, and a deepening connection with inner wisdom.

Each type of mandala offers a unique doorway to self-discovery, healing, and transformation. Whether through traditional designs, nature-inspired forms, healing intentions, personal expressions, or sacred geometries, these mandalas invite you to embark on a profound journey of self-exploration and connection to the sacred.

Chapter 9 Initiating the Meditative Journey: Detailed Practical Techniques for Symbol Meditation

In the previous chapters, we explored the profound meanings and significance of various symbols across cultures. Now, in Chapter 9, we introduce you to transformative techniques for meditating on these symbols. These methods will guide you in engaging with the transformative energies and wisdom held within each symbol, fostering inner growth and connection. Let us dive into the realm of practical symbol meditation.

Section 1: Creating a Sacred Space for Symbol Meditation

1.1 Establishing a Dedicated Space: Designate a quiet and serene space in your home or wherever you feel comfortable for your symbol meditation practice.

Clear the area of clutter and create an ambiance that supports relaxation and introspection.

1.2 Personalizing the Space: Decorate your meditation space with objects and images that resonate with the symbols you will be working with. These can include artwork, statues, or symbolic representations that evoke the essence of the symbols. Surrounding yourself with these visual reminders enhances the atmosphere and deepens your connection to the symbols.

Section 2: Seating and Posture

2.1 Finding Comfort: Choose a comfortable seating position that allows for relaxation and stability. This can be sitting cross-legged on a cushion, using a meditation bench, or sitting in a chair with your feet flat on the ground. The key is to find a position that supports an upright posture while being at ease.

2.2 Aligning the Spine: Maintain an upright posture, aligning your spine from the base to the crown of your head. Imagine a string gently pulling you upwards, elongating your spine. This alignment facilitates the flow of energy and supports mental alertness during your meditation practice.

Section 3: Focusing the Attention

3.1 Setting an Intention: Before starting your meditation, set a clear intention for your practice. This can be to deepen your connection to the symbol, gain insights, find inner balance, or cultivate specific qualities represented by the symbol. Clarifying your intention provides a focal point for your meditation and deepens the significance of the experience.

3.2 Gentle Gaze or Visualization: Direct your attention to the symbol you have chosen to work with. If the symbol is physically present, softly gaze at it, taking in its form, details, and energy. If the symbol is not physically present, close your eyes and visualize it in your mind's eye with clarity and depth. Hold your focus on the symbol throughout your meditation, allowing it to become a point of concentration and connection.

Section 4: Breathing and Centering

4.1 Conscious Breathing: Begin your meditation by focusing on your breath. Take slow, deep breaths, inhaling through your nose and exhaling through your nose. Allow your breath to be smooth and natural, without forcing it. As you inhale, visualize or feel the life-giving energy of the breath filling your body. As you exhale, release any tension or distractions, allowing yourself to become fully present.

4.2 Centering and Grounding: As you continue to breathe, bring your awareness to the center of your being. Visualize or feel a sense of grounding, connecting with the Earth's supportive energy. Imagine roots extending from the base of your spine, grounding you deeply into the Earth. This grounding practice fosters stability and a sense of rootedness during your meditation.

Section 5: Cultivating Presence and Reflection

5.1 Cultivating Presence: As you engage with the symbol, allow yourself to be fully present in the moment. Release any thoughts, judgments, or expectations that arise. Embrace a state of openness and receptivity, allowing the transformative energies of the symbol to guide your experience.

5.2 Reflective Contemplation: After your meditation, take a few moments to reflect on your experience. Journaling or quiet contemplation can help deepen your understanding of the symbol's significance in your life. Consider any insights, emotions, or sensations that arose during the meditation, and explore how they relate to your intention and personal journey.

Through the practical techniques introduced in this chapter, you are equipped to engage in symbol meditation with purpose and intention. As you embark on your meditative journey, remember that each practice is unique, and it is through regular engagement and exploration that you will discover the transformative power and wisdom that lie within these sacred symbols.

In the next chapter, we will dive deeper into the symbolism and practical applications of specific symbols from various cultural traditions, inviting you to embark on transformative journeys with each one.

Chapter 10 Guided Egyptian Symbol Meditation

Let's explore two Egyptian symbols and provide practical ways to meditate on them: the Ankh and the Eye of Horus.

Meditating on the Ankh:

Seating and Posture: Find a comfortable seated position, ensuring that your spine is upright and your body is relaxed. Place your hands on your lap or adopt a mudra that resonates with your intention.

Focusing the Attention: Gently close your eyes and bring your attention to your breath. Allow your breath to become slow, steady, and natural. With each breath, let go of any tension or distractions, and bring your awareness to the center of your being.

Visualization: Visualize the Ankh symbol with vivid clarity in your mind's eye. Observe its distinct shape, which resembles a cross with a looped top. Imagine the looped top extending upward, reaching towards the heavens, while the vertical line descends into the earth. Hold this image in your mind, embracing the symbol's essence of life and immortality.

Breathing Technique: As you continue to visualize the Ankh, synchronize your breath with its symbolism. On each inhalation, imagine the life-giving energy entering your body through the vertical line of the Ankh, infusing you with vitality and life force. As you

exhale, visualize any stagnant or negative energy being released, making way for renewal and transformation. Allow yourself to become a conduit for the universal life force, experiencing a sense on unity and connection.

Goal and Intention: The goal of meditating on the Ankh is to connect with the eternal nature of life and awaken your inner vitality. Set an intention to embrace the gift of life, to honor the interconnectedness of all living beings, and to cultivate a deep sense of gratitude for the present moment.

Meditating on the Eye of Horus:

Seating and Posture: Assume a comfortable seated position with your spine erect and your body relaxed. Rest your hands on your lap or adopt a mudra that resonates with your intention.

Focusing the Attention: Softly close your eyes and turn your attention inward. Release any tension or distractions, allowing yourself to fully immerse in the present moment. Bring your awareness to the center of your being, creating a space of stillness and receptivity.

Visualization: Visualize the Eye of Horus, also known as the Udjat or Wadjet, in your mind's eye. Observe its distinctive shape, which resembles an eye with stylized markings. Hold the image of the Eye of Horus in your mind, embracing its symbolism of protection, intuition, and spiritual insight.

Breathing Technique: With each breath, allow your breath to deepen and slow down. Imagine breathing in a bright, golden light that symbolizes the wisdom and guidance associated with the Eye of Horus. As you exhale, visualize any doubts, fears, or negative energies being released, making space for clarity and insight.

Goal and Intention: The goal of meditating on the Eye of Horus is to awaken your intuitive faculties and gain spiritual insight. Set an intention to develop a deep connection with your inner guidance, to trust your intuition, and to cultivate clarity and discernment in your life.

Remember, these meditation instructions are meant to provide a framework, but feel free to adapt them to suit your personal preferences and needs. Explore the symbolism of these Egyptian symbols, immerse yourself in their energetic essence, and allow their transformative powers to unfold within you.

Chapter 11 Guided Sri Yantra Meditation

Let's explore practical ways to meditate on one of the symbols mentioned earlier: the Sri Yantra.

Here is a step-by-step guide:

Setting the Space: Find a quiet and comfortable space where you can engage in undisturbed meditation. Create a serene ambiance by lighting candles, burning incense, or playing soft, calming music.

Seated Posture: Sit in a comfortable cross-legged position on a cushion or a chair. Ensure your spine is upright but relaxed, allowing for free flow of energy.

Breathing and Centering: Take a few deep breaths to relax your body and mind. Inhale deeply, filling your abdomen, chest, and lungs with air. Exhale slowly, releasing any tension or distractions.

Focus and Visualization: Bring the image of the Sri Yantra to your mind's eye or have a physical representation of it placed in front of you. Gaze softly at the symbol, allowing your attention to rest on its intricate geometry and interlocking triangles. Visualize the Sri Yantra as a three-dimensional object, with each layer and line coming alive and radiating vibrant energy. Picture your body in the shape of an upward facing tetrahedron. Let the interior of that shape vibrate gently while you receive a powerful sense of vitality and heightened awareness

Breath Awareness: Direct your attention to your breath while maintaining your focus on the Sri Yantra. Notice the natural rhythm of your breath, without trying to control it. Allow your breath to flow smoothly and effortlessly, anchoring you in the present moment.

Symbolic Reflection: Reflect on the symbolic qualities and meanings associated with the Sri Yantra. Contemplate its representation of balance, manifestation, and spiritual growth. Explore how these qualities resonate with your own life and spiritual journey.

Intent and Affirmation: Set a clear intention for your meditation practice with the Sri Yantra. Affirm your desire to align with the harmonious energies it embodies. Repeat a simple affirmation, such as "I open myself to the transformative energies of the Sri Yantra, inviting balance and spiritual growth into my life."

Deepening the Connection: As you continue to gaze at the Sri Yantra, imagine yourself merging with its energetic field. Feel the harmonious qualities of the symbol permeating your being, bringing balance and clarity to your thoughts, emotions, and energy centers. Visualize yourself embodying the qualities represented by the Sri Yantra, experiencing a profound sense of connection to the divine and a deepening of your spiritual journey.

Closing the Meditation: When you feel ready to conclude your meditation, take a few final deep breaths. Express gratitude for the experience and the insights gained. Slowly bring your awareness back to your surroundings, gently opening your eyes.

The goal of meditating on the Sri Yantra is to align yourself with its harmonious energies and invite balance, manifestation, and spiritual growth into your life. By focusing your attention, visualizing the symbol, and connecting with its symbolic meanings, you cultivate a deeper connection with the essence of the Sri Yantra, allowing its transformative qualities to unfold within you.

Chapter 12 Guided Mandala Meditation

Let's examine a practical way to meditate on mandalas, allowing you to experience their transformative power and find inner peace and harmony.

Prepare Your Space: Find a quiet and comfortable space where you can engage in your meditation practice. Ensure that you won't be disturbed during this time. Set up a clean and inviting area, placing a physical mandala or a printed image of a mandala in your line of sight.

Seating and Posture: Choose a seated position that allows for both relaxation and alertness. Sit on a cushion or a chair with your spine upright and your body relaxed. Rest your hands comfortably in your lap or adopt a mudra that resonates with your intention.

Focusing and Centering: Gently gaze at the central point of the mandala or the entire mandala itself. Allow your eyes to soften and your focus to settle on the intricate details and patterns. If you are using a physical mandala, let your eyes explore the symmetrical designs and colors. If you are visualizing a mandala, close your eyes and bring the image to mind, visualizing it with clarity and vibrancy.

Breath Awareness: Shift your attention to your breath, observing its natural rhythm and flow. Take a few deep breaths, inhaling slowly through your nose and exhaling through your mouth. Allow your breath to guide you into a state of relaxation and presence. As you continue, let your breath settle into a natural and gentle pattern, serving as an anchor for your focus.

Engaging with the Mandala: As you gaze at or visualize the mandala, allow yourself to be fully present in the moment. Let go of any thoughts, distractions, or expectations, and surrender to the experience. Explore the intricate details, colors, and shapes of the mandala. Notice the sensations and emotions that arise as you engage with its energy. Allow the mandala to draw you deeper into its transformative qualities.

Reflection and Contemplation: As you continue to engage with the mandala, observe any thoughts, feelings, or insights that arise within you. Reflect on the symbolism and patterns present in the mandala. Consider how they relate to your own life, challenges, and aspirations. Allow the mandala to become a mirror for self-reflection and contemplation, inviting a deeper understanding of your inner world.

Integration and Closing: When you feel ready, gently shift your focus away from the mandala. Take a few moments to express gratitude for the experience and the wisdom gained. Slowly bring your awareness back to the physical space around you, wiggling your fingers and toes, and taking a deep breath. Allow yourself a moment of quiet reflection before resuming your daily activities.

Chapter 13 Practical Flower Of Life Meditation

Let's explore a practical way to meditate on the symbol of the Flower of Life, a sacred geometric pattern known for its representation of interconnectedness and the infinite expansion of consciousness.

Preparation: Find a quiet and comfortable space where you can sit undisturbed for the duration of your meditation. Assume a comfortable seated position, either on a cushion or a chair, with your back straight and relaxed. Close your eyes and take a few deep breaths, allowing yourself to settle into a state of calm and relaxation.

Meditation Steps: Focus on the Breath: Begin by bringing your attention to your breath. Take slow, deep breaths, inhaling through your nose and exhaling through your mouth. Allow your breath to be smooth and effortless, cultivating a sense of relaxation and presence.

Visualize the Flower of Life: With your eyes closed, bring the image of the Flower of Life to your mind's eye. Imagine its intricate overlapping circles and the symmetrical patterns they create. Visualize the vibrant energy emanating from the center of the symbol and expanding outward, encompassing your entire field of awareness.

Contemplate Interconnectedness: As you hold the image of the Flower of Life in your mind, reflect on its representation of interconnectedness. Contemplate how each circle is linked to the others, forming a harmonious whole. Consider how this symbol mirrors the interconnected nature of existence, from the microcosm to the macrocosm. Allow yourself to sense the profound unity that permeates all things.

Align with Expansion: As you continue to focus on the Flower of Life, allow yourself to align with the infinite expansion of consciousness that it represents. Visualize your own awareness expanding, transcending the boundaries of your physical body and merging with the vast expanse of the universe. Embrace the boundless potential that lies within you and the interconnectedness of all existence.

Maintain Presence and Awareness: Throughout the meditation, maintain a state of presence and heightened awareness. If your mind wanders, gently bring your attention back to the symbol and the sensations it evokes within you. Embrace a sense of curiosity and openness, allowing the meditation to unfold naturally.

Breath Integration: As you approach the end of your meditation, bring your focus back to your breath. Observe the rhythm of your inhalations and exhalations, grounding yourself in the present moment. Take a few deep breaths, inhaling gratitude and exhaling any tension or distractions.

Closing and Integration: Slowly open your eyes and take a moment to reflect on your meditation experience. Notice any insights or sensations that arose during the practice. Consider how the contemplation of the Flower of Life has deepened your understanding of interconnectedness and expansion. Carry this awareness with you as you move throughout your day, integrating the transformative energies of the symbol into your life.

The goal of this meditation is to cultivate a deeper sense of interconnectedness, expansion, and unity. By engaging with the symbol of the Flower of Life in this way, you align your consciousness with its inherent qualities, inviting transformative insights and a heightened sense of awareness into your life. Regular practice can deepen your understanding of these principles and facilitate personal growth and spiritual awakening.

Chapter 14 Guided 64 Tetrahedron Grid Meditation

Meditation Exercise: Awakening Consciousness with the 64 Tetrahedron Grid

The 64 Tetrahedron Grid, also known as the Star Tetrahedron, is a geometric structure consisting of interlocking tetrahedrons. This meditation exercise is designed to help you explore and activate the transformative energy of the 64 Tetrahedron Grid. Find a quiet and comfortable space where you can engage in this practice without distractions.

Preparation: Sit in a comfortable position, ensuring that your spine is straight and your body is relaxed. Take a few deep breaths to center yourself and bring your awareness to the present moment.
Close your eyes and allow your body and mind to settle into a state of calm.

Cultivating Awareness: Begin by bringing your attention to your breath. Observe the natural flow of your breath, without trying to control it. Gradually shift your awareness to the physical sensations of your body, noticing any areas of tension or relaxation. Take a few moments to consciously release any tension you may be holding, allowing your body to relax further.

Visualizing the 64 Tetrahedron Grid: Envision a vibrant and radiant 64 Tetrahedron Grid surrounding your entire being. Visualize each tetrahedron in the grid as a shimmering, translucent pyramid with equilateral triangular faces. Picture the interlocking tetrahedrons forming a three-dimensional star-like structure, emanating a powerful and harmonious energy.

Activating the Grid: Imagine a stream of pure, white light descending from above, flowing into the topmost tetrahedron of the grid. Visualize this divine light permeating the entire grid, illuminating each tetrahedron with its radiant energy. As the light fills the grid, sense its transformative and healing vibrations expanding within and around you.

Merging with the Grid: Intentionally align your own energy field with the energy of the 64 Tetrahedron Grid.
Envision your consciousness expanding and merging with the grid, becoming one with its transformative power.
Allow yourself to feel the interconnectedness of your being with the infinite energy and wisdom encapsulated within the grid.

Receiving Insights and Healing: Open yourself to receive insights, guidance, and healing as you remain in a state of connection with the grid. Listen to the whispers of your inner wisdom, allowing any thoughts, images, or sensations to arise without judgment. Trust in the transformative energy of the grid to facilitate personal growth, expanded awareness, and profound healing.

Gratitude and Integration: When you feel ready, express gratitude for the experience and the wisdom gained during the meditation. Slowly bring your awareness back to your breath and the sensations of your body. Gently open your eyes, take a moment to ground yourself, and carry the energetic imprint of the 64 Tetrahedron Grid with you into your daily life. Practice this meditation regularly to deepen your connection with the transformative energy of the 64 Tetrahedron Grid. As you explore and integrate this sacred geometry into your being, observe the shifts in consciousness, increased awareness, and enhanced spiritual growth that may arise.

Chapter 15 Guided Tree of Life Meditation

Preparation: Find a quiet and comfortable space where you can sit or lie down in a relaxed position. Take a few deep breaths to center yourself and let go of any tension or distractions. Close your eyes and allow your mind to settle into a state of calmness.

Setting the Intention: Bring your awareness to the symbol of the Tree of Life, visualizing it in your mind's eye. Set your intention for the meditation, such as seeking insight, balance, or connection to higher realms. Affirm your readiness to explore the different aspects of the Tree of Life and its symbolic meanings.

Grounding and Centering: Imagine roots extending from the soles of your feet, sinking deep into the earth.

Visualize these roots anchoring you firmly, grounding your energy, and connecting you to the stability and nourishment of the Earth.

Tree Visualization: Visualize yourself as a magnificent tree, with your body as the trunk and branches reaching upward. See the Tree of Life superimposed upon your own form, aligning its sephiroth (spheres) with the corresponding energy centers within your body.

Sephiroth Exploration: Start at the base of your tree, connecting with the sephira of Malkuth, representing the physical realm. Take a moment to sense your connection to the Earth, grounding and stabilizing your energy. Gradually ascend through the sephiroth, spending time with each one. As you move upward, focus on the qualities, colors, and energies associated with each sephira. Explore the sephiroth of Yesod, Hod, Netzach, Tiphereth, Geburah, Chesed, Binah, and Chokmah, allowing yourself to experience their unique energies and symbolism. Finally, reach the pinnacle of the tree, the sephira of Kether, representing divine unity and transcendence. Connect with the infinite and expansive energy of the divine.

Symbolic Reflection: Take a few moments to reflect on the journey through the Tree of Life and the experiences you encountered at each sephira. Notice any insights, emotions, or sensations that arise as you explore the different aspects of the tree. Allow yourself to integrate these experiences, recognizing the interconnectedness of the various energies within and around you.

Gratitude and Closing: Express gratitude for the wisdom and guidance received during the meditation. Slowly bring your awareness back to your physical body, feeling the sensations of your breath and the surface beneath you.

Gently open your eyes and take a moment to ground yourself before resuming your day. Remember, this meditation technique is just a guide. Feel free to adapt it based on your personal preferences and experiences. Regular practice with the Tree of Life meditation can deepen your connection to its symbolic power, bringing insight, balance, and a sense of unity with the greater cosmic forces.

Chapter 16 The Science of Meditation and Symbol Engagement: Unveiling the Transformative Power

In this chapter, we take a look at fascinating scientific research that sheds light on the profound effects of meditation and symbol engagement on our minds, bodies, and overall well-being. By exploring the scientific underpinnings of these practices, we deepen our understanding of their transformative power and gain a broader perspective on their potential impact on humanity.

Section 1: The Neurobiology of Meditation

1.1 Brain Plasticity: Meditation and symbol engagement can induce neuroplasticity; the brain's ability to reorganize and form new neural connections. Research suggests that regular meditation practice can lead to structural and functional changes in the brain, enhancing attention, emotional regulation, and cognitive abilities.

1.2 Emotional Well-being: Studies have demonstrated the impact of meditation on stress reduction and emotional well-being. By engaging with symbols and meditative practices, individuals can experience reduced levels of stress, anxiety, and depression, along with increased resilience and emotional balance. Meditation has long been recognized as a powerful tool for reducing stress and promoting emotional well-being. Numerous studies have investigated the effects of meditation on the body's stress response, emotional regulation, and overall mental health. In this section, we delve into the research that highlights the transformative impact of meditation on stress reduction and emotional well-being.

1.3 Stress Reduction:

Research studies consistently demonstrate that regular meditation practice can significantly reduce stress levels. A meta-analysis published in (2014) reviewed 47 trials and found that meditation interventions were associated with reduced anxiety, depression, and stress. The practice of meditation helps activate the body's relaxation response, reducing the release of stress hormones and promoting a state of calmness and tranquility.

1.4 Emotional Regulation:

Meditation practices have been shown to enhance emotional regulation skills, allowing individuals to manage and navigate their emotions more effectively. A study published in (2012) revealed that mindfulness meditation enhanced cognitive reappraisal, the ability to reframe and reinterpret emotional experiences, resulting in improved emotional well-being. By cultivating present-moment awareness and non-reactivity, meditation empowers individuals to respond to emotions with greater clarity and equanimity.

1.5 Enhanced Resilience:

Meditation plays a vital role in building resilience—the ability to bounce back from life's challenges. Studies have shown that regular meditation practice can increase psychological resilience by reducing the impact of stressors and improving coping mechanisms. One study in (2013) found that mindfulness meditation training decreased emotional and physiological reactivity to stress, leading to greater resilience in the face of adversity.

1.6 Improved Mood and Well-being:

Meditation has been linked to improved mood and overall psychological well-being. Research has demonstrated that mindfulness-based interventions effectively reduced symptoms of depression and enhanced well-being in individuals with mood disorders. Meditation practices promote self-awareness, self-compassion, and the cultivation of positive emotions, contributing to a more positive outlook on life.

1.7 Neuroplasticity and Emotional Regulation:

Studies using neuroimaging techniques, such as functional magnetic resonance imaging (fMRI), have shown that meditation can induce changes in brain structure and function, particularly in regions associated with emotion regulation. The practice of meditation has been found to increase gray matter density in the prefrontal cortex, the amygdala, and the hippocampus, promoting emotional regulation, attentional control, and overall emotional well-being.

Through consistent meditation practice, individuals can experience a profound reduction in stress levels, improved emotional regulation, increased resilience, enhanced mood, and overall emotional well-being. The transformative impact of meditation on stress reduction and emotional well-being underscores its immense potential as a tool for cultivating inner peace, balance, and psychological flourishing.

Section 2: Cognitive Benefits of Symbol Engagement

2.1 Attention and Concentration: Research suggests that sustained visual focus on symbols can enhance cognitive control, working memory, and sustained attention, leading to improved cognitive performance in various tasks.

2.2 Creativity and Insight: Engagement with symbols can stimulate creative thinking and insight generation. Studies indicate that symbol engagement can enhance divergent thinking, problem-solving abilities, and the generation of novel ideas, fostering greater creativity and innovation.

Section 3: Emotional and Psychological Well-being

3.1 Self-Reflection and Self-Awareness: By engaging with symbols, individuals can gain insight into their thoughts, emotions, and patterns of behavior, leading to greater self-understanding, acceptance, and personal growth.

3.2 Empathy and Compassion: Research suggests that engaging with symbols representing unity and interconnectedness can enhance feelings of compassion, altruism, and a sense of social connectedness.

Section 4: Mind-Body Connection

4.1 Stress Reduction and Physical Health: Meditation and symbol engagement can positively impact physical health and well-being. Studies indicate that these practices can lower blood pressure, reduce inflammation, boost the immune system, and promote overall cardiovascular health, contributing to improved physical well-being.

4.2 Psychoneuroimmunology: In the field of psychoneuroimmunology and its research on the intricate connection between mind, emotions, and the immune system. We see studies that suggest meditation and symbol engagement can influence immune function, promoting a balanced immune response and overall wellness.

Section 5: The Power of Symbolic Engagement

5.1 Archetypal Psychology: Through the work of Carl Jung and the concept of archetypes in symbol engagement we can begin to contemplate the collective unconscious and the symbolism inherent in our psyche, we investigate how engaging with symbols can unlock deep layers of meaning, fostering personal growth, and spiritual transformation.

5.2 Transpersonal Psychology: By engaging with symbols in meditation, individuals can access transpersonal realms, experience expanded states of awareness, and tap into the interconnectedness of all beings.

By exploring the science behind meditation and symbol engagement, we uncover the remarkable ways in which these practices can positively impact our minds, bodies, and overall well-being. The scientific research invites us to embrace these transformative practices with confidence and inspires us to further explore their potential for personal growth, social connection, and collective evolution.

Chapter 17 Reflections on the Sacred Journey: Insights and Transformations

In our exploration of visual meditation using symbols and sacred geometry, we have embarked on a profound journey of self-discovery, connection, and transformation. As we approach the culmination of this book, let us engage in introspection, embracing the profound insights gained and the transformative experiences that have unfolded throughout our journey.

Section 1: Awakening to Unity and Interconnectedness

Through the practice of harnessing the power of symbols and sacred geometry, we have come to realize the inherent unity and interconnectedness of all things. As we delved into the intricate patterns and harmonious forms, we witnessed how they mirror the underlying fabric of the universe itself. These experiences have opened our hearts and minds to the realization that we are not separate, but rather integral parts of a vast cosmic tapestry.

Section 2: Expansion of Consciousness and Self-Discovery

Engaging with sacred geometry in meditation has expanded our consciousness and allowed us to access deeper realms within ourselves. Through contemplation and visualization, we have tapped into dormant potentials, awakened our intuition, and gained insights that transcend the limitations of our everyday awareness. This exploration has been a journey of self-discovery, guiding us to uncover the hidden facets of our being and empowering us to embrace our true essence.

Section 3: Harmonizing Balance and Integration

The transformative power of visual meditation on symbols and sacred geometry has brought us into harmonious balance. As we immersed ourselves in the sacred forms, we experienced the integration of polarities within ourselves—the union of the masculine and feminine, the reconciliation of light and shadow, and the harmonization of opposing forces. This balance has expanded beyond our meditation practice, permeating our daily lives and relationships, fostering a deep sense of harmony within and without.

Section 4: Spiritual Awakening and Transcendence

Through the practice of engaging with these transformative energies, we have touched the realms of the divine, transcending the limitations of the material world. We have felt the whispers of universal wisdom, the subtle nudges of cosmic forces, and the expansive presence of the sacred. This awakening has ignited the flame of our own inner divinity, reminding us of our inherent connection to something greater than ourselves.

Section 5: Integration and Continuing the Journey

The insights gained and the transformations experienced are meant to be integrated into our daily lives and continued on our personal and spiritual journeys. We carry the wisdom and the energy of sacred geometry within us, allowing it to guide us as we navigate the ever-unfolding path of self-discovery and growth.

Conclusion

As we reach the culmination of our journey through the portals of transcendence, we reflect upon the profound discoveries and transformative experiences that have unfolded within these pages. The exploration of symbols has provided us with a window into the vast tapestry of human consciousness, offering glimpses of ancient wisdom and the universal truths that resonate within our souls.

Throughout this book, we have explored the rich history, meanings, and practical applications of symbols as gateways to expanded awareness and inner transformation. We have witnessed how the power of imagery, combined with focused intention and contemplative practice, can awaken dormant potentials, deepen our spiritual connections, and bring forth profound insights and healing.

In our quest to understand the significance of symbols, we have recognized their ability to transcend cultural and temporal boundaries. From the sacred geometries of ancient civilizations to the modern archetypes emerging from the collective unconscious, symbols continue to serve as bridges that unite humanity's collective spiritual heritage.

Through the practices of visual meditation, we have learned to harness the potency of symbols, to infuse them with personal meaning, and to cultivate a sacred space within our hearts and minds. We have embraced the art of mindful contemplation, allowing these symbols to guide us on journeys of self-discovery, unlocking the depths of our being and nurturing our connection to the divine.

However, this is not the end but rather a new beginning, a stepping stone on your ongoing journey of spiritual evolution. As you close this book, remember that the wisdom and transformative power of symbols remain ever accessible, waiting to be engaged with and integrated into your daily life.

Continue to explore the symbols that resonate with you, for they are gateways to infinite possibilities. Allow them to infuse your meditation practice, to inspire your creative expression, and to serve as reminders of the profound truths that reside within you and in the world around you.

Remember that the magic lies not only in the symbols themselves but also in your willingness to engage with them authentically and with an open heart. Embrace the beauty of your own unique experiences and interpretations, for each individual's journey with symbols is a personal and sacred dance with the divine.

May the wisdom gleaned from this exploration of visual meditation on symbols continue to guide you, inspire you, and foster a deep sense of interconnectedness with all of existence. As you navigate the vast landscapes of consciousness, may these symbols be your steadfast companions, illuminating your path and awakening the inherent divinity that resides within you.

With heartfelt gratitude for joining me on this profound exploration, I bid you farewell for now. As you step forward on your continued spiritual journey, may you carry the transformative power of visual meditation on symbols with you, allowing it to radiate love, light, and awakening wherever your path may lead.

In the final section of "Portals of Transcendence" I invite you to initiate a captivating visual journey through the rich symbolism we have explored throughout the book. Here, the wisdom of sacred symbols comes to life through a collection of beautifully illustrated images.

These illustrations function as a visual bridge, enabling you to forge a deeper connection with the symbolic realm and enhancing your meditation practice. As you navigate this visual journey, I encourage you to discern and embrace the symbols that resonate with you personally. May your sacred voyage be adorned with infinite blessings, abundant joy, and boundless love.

Kevin Little

ANKH

SOMETIMES REFERRED TO AS THE KEY OF LIFE.
REPRESENTATIVE OF ETERNAL LIFE IN ANCIENT EGYPT

EYE OF HORUS

BELIEVED TO HAVE PROTECTIVE MAGICAL POWER

SRI YANTRA

CONSISTS OF 9 INTERLOCKING TRIANGLES. 4 UPWARD
ONES WHICH REPRESENT SHIVA, AND 5 DOWNWARD ONES
REPRESENTING SHAKTI. ALL THESE SURROUND THE
CENTRAL POINT, THE BINDU. THESE TRIANGLES
REPRESENT THE COSMOS AND THE HUMAN BODY.

FLOWER OF LIFE

DEMONSTRATED REPEATING MATHEMATICAL PATTERNS
THAT EXIST IN NATURE AND THE UNIVERSE AT LARGE.

METATRON'S CUBE

CONTAINS THE 5 KEY SHAPES THAT MAKE UP ALL MATTER IN THE UNIVERSE. KNOWN AS THE PLATONIC SOLIDS, THEY ARE THE STAR TETRAHEDRON, HEXAHEDRON, OCTAHEDRON, DODECAHEDRON, AND ICOSAHEDRON.

VESICA PISCIS

SOME BELIEVE THE VESICA PISCIS IS A SYMBOL OF THE
DIVINE FEMININE. SEEN AS THE MOTHER OF GEOMETRIC
SHAPES GIVING BIRTH TO THE TRIANGLE, SQUARE AND
OTHER REGULAR POLYGONS.

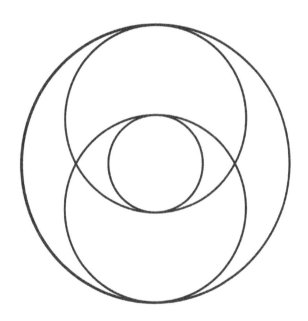

MERKABA

REPRESENTS THE PATH OF ASCENSION TOWARDS HIGHER
DIMENSIONS.

TREE OF LIFE

REPRESENTS THE DESCENT OF THE DIVINE INTO THE
MANIFEST WORLD AND METHODS BY WHICH THE DIVINE UNION
MAY BE ATTAINED IN THIS LIFE.

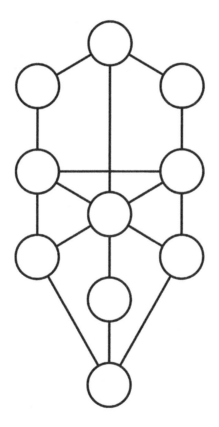

64 GRID TETRAHEDRON

ALSO KNOWN AS THE GRID OF LIFE. SOME SAY
SYMBOLIZES THE ESSENSE OF LIFE.

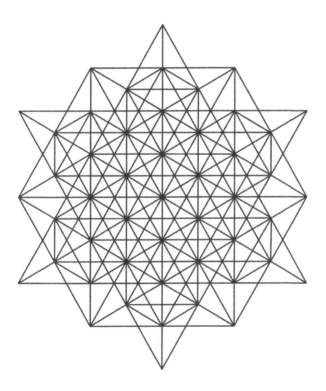

CUBOCTAHEDRON

THE MOST PRIMARY GEOMETRIC ENERGY
ARRAY IN THE COSMOS

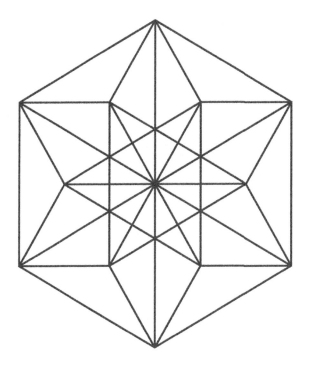

SEED OF LIFE

SYMBOLIZES THAT ALL LIFE ORIGINATED FROM A
SINGLE SOURCE IN A DIVINE PLAN

FIBONACCI SEQUENCE

FOUND IN NATURE THE GOLDEN RATIO OF
1.61803399

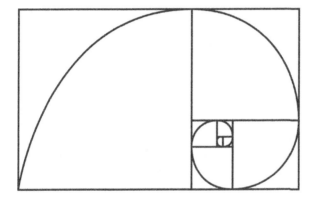

TORUS

SYMBOL OF THE CONTINOUS CYCLE OF CREATION AND
DESTRUCTION

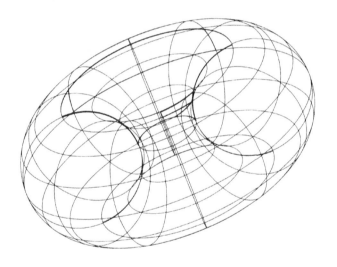

Made in the USA
Las Vegas, NV
14 April 2024

88691660R00075